HAIKU SMILES

NANCY LEE SHRADER

ALL THINGS THAT MATTER
PRESS

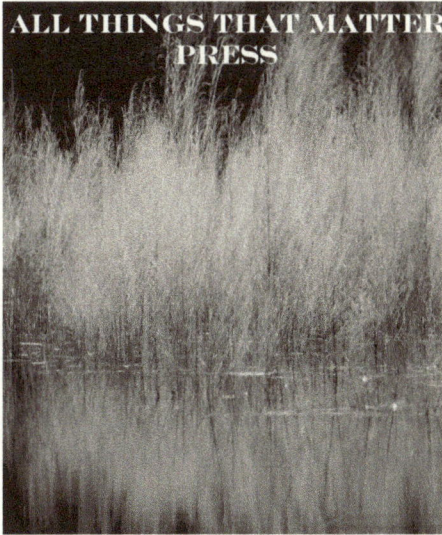

HAIKU SMILES

ISBN: 09822-056-5-1

ISBN13: 978-0-9822056-5-5

LIBRARY OF CONGRESS NUMBER: 2008941794

COVER DESIGN BY ALL THINGS THAT MATTER PRESS

PUBLISHED IN 2008 BY ALL THINGS THAT MATTER PRESS

PRINTED IN THE UNITED STATES OF AMERICA

Table of Contents

Introduction

To those of you who are not familiar with the Haiku form of poetry. I will give you a little back ground, so you will understand this form of writing.

Haiku is a poetic form and a type of poetry from the Japanese culture. Haiku combines form, content, and language in a meaningful, yet compact form. Haiku poets write about everyday things. Many themes include nature, feelings, or experiences. Usually they use simple words and grammar. The most common form for Haiku is three short lines. The first line usually contains five (5) syllables. Haiku doesn't rhyme. A Haiku must paint a mental image in the reader's mind. This is the challenge of Haiku – to put the poem's meaning and imagery in the reader's mind in ONLY 17 SYLLABLES over just three (3) lines of poetry!

My first poem in Haiku Smiles titled Haiku Seasons is eight Haiku poems that stand alone, but also when strung together stand together as one poem. I hope you will enjoy reading Haiku Smiles as much as I did writing them.

Haiku Seasons

Leaves fall in colors
Orange, yellow red and gold
Summer's afterglow

Autumn sings its song
In musical crackling sounds
Robins fly away

Winter winds blow hard
Icy cold on crystal lakes
Freezing young and old

Icicles glinting
Wrapped around in sparkling style
Glimmering daggers

Budding bursting forth
Rose awake from winter's bed
Sing a song of spring

A kaleidoscope
Colorful sweet aroma
Flowers bud, Bees sting

Summer's heat burns hot
Wilts everything all around
Grass and graceful rose

Dolphins, whales and more
Waves roll in on distant shores
Gnashing teeth destroy

Carousel of Life

$\mathscr{C}$

Carousel of life
Broadens the mind completely
Embraces the air

Amazing Grace

A

God's amazing grace
Envelopes the pure green earth
Flowers, trees blooming

Journey

J

Journey into fall
My faith springs eternally
God's love surrounds me

Puzzle Complete

P

Puzzle complete me
In gardens of love I find
My heart's missing piece

Hourglass

H

Hourglass of life
Trapping time in a bottle
Spring's fleeting moments

Rhapsody Divine

R

Rhapsody divine
Spilling on springtime with love
Ecstasy revealed

Blair Mountain

B

Above Blair Mountain
Coal wars erupt in the air
Touching innocence

Embracing the Dawn

E

Hearts are intertwined
Amazing love fills the air
Embracing the dawn

Little Goblins

L

Autumn feast tonight
Jack-O-Lanterns light the night
Little goblins treat

Fifth Place
Nancy Lee Shrader - Little Goblins
October 13, 2008

Sounds of Autumn

S

Sounds of autumn leaves
Break the silence of the night
Crunching underfoot

Honorable Mention
Nancy Lee Shrader - Sounds of Autumn
October 13, 2008

Autumn Moon

A

Autumn moon looms high
Large and orange in disguise
Coloring the leaves

Cat in the Pumpkins

C

Cats in the pumpkins
Hides inside Jack-O-Lantern
Giving all a scare

Second Place

Nancy Lee Shrader - Cats in the Pumpkins

November 11, 2008

Cat Dance

C

Under autumn moon
Black cats dance on Halloween
Hear the children laugh

Pumpkin Pies

P

Pumpkins on parade
Celebrate this Thanksgiving
Pumpkin Pies Yum! Yum!

Fruitcake

F

Candied fruit and nuts
All rolled up in sweet design
Holiday Fruit Cake

I'm Alive

I

Hear me, I'm alive
I'm buried in the dark earth
A bulb calls for help

Devils Bluff

D

Ghosts on Devils Bluff
Find Mayweather House a curse
They moan in the night

Demon's Claw

D

Demon's claw ripping
Unbridled lusting for blood
Flesh torn from the bone

Demons

D

Demons darkened gloom
Whispers tell me to get out
Coming from the tomb

Hunters Beware

H

You hunters beware
Fall breezes carry the scent
Thanksgiving table

Pumpkin Dance

P

Dance of the pumpkins
Rows of pumpkin perfection
Thanksgiving parade

Haiku First Place

Nancy Lee Shrader - Pumpkin Dance

Spell

S

Curse upon your love
My spell cannot be broken
Your heart turned to stone

Young Hands

Y

In a wooded glen
Boy Scout kneeling by a stump
Young hands tie the knots

Ballerina Fair

B

Ballerina fair
Dances on her tippy toes
Catching moonbeams glow

Forever Blended

F

Forever blended
Springtime and summer collide
Hope springs eternal

Stars Fall

S

Stars fall from the sky
Giving hope to the hopeless
Lights my darkened night

Celestial Skies

C

In celestial skies
In the Lord's heavenly realm
Jesus calls my name

God's Decree

G

God sent His decree
A maiden, lamb and a rule
Mary bore Jesus

Shroud

S

A man wears a shroud
Resurrected from the dead
Life springs eternal

Seventh Place

Nancy Lee Shrader - The Shroud

Anger Swells

A

Girl and lamb at school
Laughing fills the air this day
Teacher's anger swells

Emerald Eyes

E

Her emerald sad eyes
Glistening with tears falling
Down her cheeks like rain

Sand Dunes

S

Sand dunes of the mind
Too often catch us off guard
Left sandstorms behind

Mirror Reflection

M

Picked from the garden
Flowers now have a new home
Mirror Reflection

Cloistered

C

Cloistered in the cave
Far away from prying eyes
Jaguar tends her young

Trellis

Trellis of the Heart
Weaves the vines of love's embrace
Thorns are captured there

Drizzle

D

Clouds collide in tune
Rain becomes freezing drizzle
Treacherous roadway

Caustic

C

Caustic rivers run
Deceitful rocks hide below
Corroding the shore

Ravine

$$\mathcal{R}$$

Ravine of sadness
Envelops body and soul
Rips at the heart's core

Verdant

V

Verdant garden thrives
In the summer's afterglow
Harvest on the wind

Lullaby

L

Winter's lullaby
Seedlings sleep under the snow
In Nature's nursery

Tousled

T

Tousled by the wind
Leaves flying thither yonder
Hear the crackling sound

Secular

S

Secular movement
They are wiping out God's Word
Christians take a stand

Everglades

E

Death stalks murky green
Alligator seeks its prey
Everglades plunder

Eagle's Wings

E

A bird warns the mouse
Danger, in the air
Swoop on eagle's wings

Bark of the Dogwood

B

Bark of the dogwood
Silent in the break of dawn
So peaceful at night

Mulberry Bush

M

Hot sun breezes blow
Mulberry bush by the creek
Wilting in the heat

Crystal Lake

C

Crystal Lake in spring
On water lilies they sing
A frog croaking song

Crystal Wonderland

C

Crystal wonderland
Trees shimmer on crystal ice
Sings a winter song

Honorable Mention

Nancy Lee Shrader - Crystal Wonderland
October 22, 2008

Island Palm

I

Island palm swaying
Coconuts fall to the ground
A loud cracking sound

Snow Angel

S

On Crystal Lake there
Snow angels breathe frosty breeze
Skating on the ice

Fifth Place

Nancy Lee Shrader - Snow Angels
October 22, 2008

Winter Flight

W

Santa's sleigh takes flight
Over a blanket of snow
Good children aware

Second Place

Nancy Lee Shrader - Winter Flight
October 22, 2008

Tribute to Winter

T

Tribute to winter
Ice skating on frozen pond
Snow ball fights, sleigh rides

Snowman at Play

S

A snowman at play
Ripples the hillsides with glee
Snow mounds in his wake

Honorable Mention

Nancy Lee Shrader - Snowman at Play
October 22, 2008

Winter Sleeps

W

Frozen terrain sleeps
Wonderland of ice and snow
Winter's lullaby

Third Place

Nancy Lee Shrader - Winter Sleeps
October 22, 2008

Santa Claus

S

Fat jolly ole elf
Takes flight one night of the year
Kneels at the manger

Rudolph

R

Rudolph's nose shines bright
Lighting Santa on his way
Every Christmas Eve

Valentine's Day

V

Hearts in the moment
Find love on Valentine's Day
Whispers sweet nothings

Clutter

C

In a closet full
Life can clutter to the brim
Do Spring Cleaning Soon!

Mystery

M

Edgar Allan Poe
Spins a tale of Mystery
Raven knocks no more

Indian Summer

I

Indian boy learns
Once a corn stalk, now peace pipe
Indian summer

Ballerina Light

B

Blinking on and off
Dance fireflies on moonlit nights
Ballerina light

Nectar

N

Down in the garden
A cup of peach nectar sweet
Be kissed by the sun

Brambles

B

Brambles and bushes
Deep within the forest green
Doe and fawn bed down

Caw! Caw!

C

In wheat field yonder
I hear the crow's haunting song
Caw! Caw! He squawks on

Tadpole

T

Itsy Bitsy frogs
In the river with no legs
Tadpole swim, swim, swim

Vale

V

In the vale I cry
Remembering love's sweet song
Winds of time transcend

Blush

B

The blush on the rose
Sending shivers down her spine
Catches in her throat

Sunbeams

S

Gentle breezes blow
String beans grow in the garden
Sunbeams kiss the rose

God's Eye

G

Beyond Heaven's Gates
On His throne where no one sees
God's eyes embrace me

Hope

H

Stars fall from the sky
Giving hope to the hopeless
Lights my darkened night

Ballerinas of the Breeze

B

Under the birch tree
Ballerinas of the Breeze
The butterflies dance

Acorn

A

Under tree yonder
Deep inside the forest green
Squirrel finds an acorn

Surrender

S

I surrender all
Into Thy Hands Lord I pray
Take my guilt away

Evening Sky

E

Stars in evening sky
Essence in splendor design
Sparkles in the mind

Fairytale in Ice

$\mathcal{F}$

Sculpture winter snow
Shaping intricate designs
Fairytale in ice

Falling Petals

F

Falling petals float
Delicately through ages
Softly in the mind

Waterfall

W

Waterfall glistens
In foamy aggression style
Beautiful danger

Crimson

C

Dances in crimson
Roses blush in the garden
Embarrassing spring

Third Place

Nancy Lee Shrader - Crimson
October 31

Sentry

S

Sentry guard awaits
Praying Mantas in silence
A predator lurks

Angel's Wings

A

Wings unfurled bow low
Gently picking wild flowers
Spreading wings take flight

Her Wand

H

Mother Nature's wand
Sprinkles fairy dust with dew
Feeds her budding rose

Whippoorwill Song

W

Whippoorwill singing
Sweet harmony in the breeze
A magical tune

Forbidden Fruit

F

A forbidden fruit
In the midst of the garden
Apple in Eve's hand

Rainbow

R

Air brushed in the sky
Kaleidoscope of color
Painted by God's hand

Daffodils

D

Perfumed aroma
Daffodils in springtime bloom
Sweet essence breezing

Morning Glories

M

Swaying in the breeze
Morning Glories in springtime
Fills my afternoon

Galilean Sea

G

Grapes kissed by the sun
By the Galilean sea
Water into wine

Summer

S

Dreaming of summer
Hot afternoons, lazy nights
Fireflies dance in rhymes

Spring

S

Spring dance of the soul
Kaleidoscope of color
Drifting in the mind

Life's Blood

L

Sap, a tree's life blood
Flowing from root into leaf
Creation of life

Paws

P

Paws on the carpet
Kitty cats and puppy dogs
Run around and play

Fawn

F

Fawn in the meadow
Whimsically frolicking
Romps with wild flowers

Complements

C

In the twilight sky
Sun complements Mister Moon
Moonbeams glow so bright

Afterglow

A

Stream in my heart stings
Rippling along so slow
Waters afterglow

Alfalfa

A

Where does hay come from?
Alfalfa grows in the field
Dry and lashed in bales

Fangs

F

Deep in forest green
Hidden in a web of fear
Fangs dripping venom

Mail Call

M

Mail call in springtime
Love letters filled with starlight
On this sunny day

New Birth Duet

N

Robin and his mate
Sing a duet on the breeze
Announcing new birth

Camouflage

C

Chameleon hides there
Camouflage, leafy cover
Hidden in plain sight

Shadow

S

Shadow in the rain
Cascading from golden moon
Its light refracted

Ebony Spider

E

Ebony spider
Spins a web of silken lace
A magical weave

Furrows

$\mathscr{F}$

Mounds in the cornfield
Mole furrows deep underground
Safe from farmers hoe

Symphony

S

Melody Rings true
A musical masterpiece
Springtime's Symphony

Plum

P

Winter knows Jack well
His finger stuck in a pie
Plum purple was he

Sleepy Head

S

Soft clover pillow
Fawn lays down his sleepy head
Dreams of playful days

His Fill

H

Rabbit in the grain
He's eating his fill today
Gardner didn't see

Falcon

F

Falcon swoop down low
Has mouse within its clutches
Carries back to nest

Summer Breezes

S

Summer breezes blow
Resonated Harmony
Music to my ears

Spring Palette

P

Wild Flowers Blooming
A kaleidoscope palette
God creates the scene

Heavenly Hues

H

A painted garden
Appeared from Earth's silent hush
God's heavenly hues

God's Hand

G

On cool afternoons
Meander through the garden
Painted by God's hand

Touched

T

Tall pine spires upward
Hopes to reach into the clouds
Be touched by God's hand

Kaleidoscope Style

K

Rainbows in sunshine
Shimmer in colors galore
Kaleidoscope style

Tidal Waves

T

Tidal waves destroy
Bringing suffering to all
A watery grave

Nature's Ice Sculpture

N

Nature's Ice Sculpture
Giant wave frozen in time
Damage Minimal

Tornados

T

Tornados whirling
Funnel clouds touching the ground
Feel natures revenge

Ocean Breeze

O

Waves of calming sea
Harmonizes nature's song
Sings on ocean breeze

Hurricane

H

Angry winds blow hard
A tropical storm rages
Typhoon blowing in

Crescent Moon

C

Beneath crescent moon
Quiet whispers feel the gloss
Glitters in the heart

Blue Horizon

B

Many different hues
In vivid combinations
A shading with flair

Crystal Blue Persuasion

C

Rippling waters
In crystal blue persuasion
Gloss my sky blue mind

Reindeer Bells

R

Imagine my dreams
Coloring me Christmas red
Wearing reindeer bells

Apples

A

Apples on the tree
Johnny Appleseed beware
Fried pies on the stove

Innocence

J

Innocence in rhyme
Sugar spice, puppy dog tails
Purity dwells here

Childhood Days

C

Childhood days galore
With ring around the rosy
Hop Scotch and Jump Rope

Sun's Afterglow

S

On hot summer nights
Stars lodge in sun's afterglow
They twinkle and shine

Time

T

Time in a bottle
Counts life down tick tock, tick tock
Time is marching on

Pandemonium

P

Chaos all around
Confusion screams in the mind
Pandemonium

Reproduction

R

Garden's flower dance
Stamen and stigma unite
Plants reproduction

God's Graphics

$$\mathcal{G}$$

In nature's garden
Needs no computer image
God's graphics with flair

Chocolate Splatters

C

Love' sweet ecstasy
Splatters erupt in the heart
With candy kisses

Rebound Love

R

Love on the rebound
Love on the run, love in haste
Love is out the gate

Shadows of Love

S

Stand in the shadows
Feeling the sun and the rain
Hear whispers of love

Rose

R

Rose of the morning
Sweet aroma in the air
Brighten up the day

Rose Heart

R

Roses fill the heart
Oh see the magic they bring
Our love intertwined

Enchanted

E

Stars up in the sky
Enchanted in the moment
Holding love so near

Endless Nights

E

Stabs at our heart's core
Praying for morning to come
End this endless night

God's Grace

G

God's amazing grace
Envelopes my inner soul
Grace fills up my heart

Alms

A

Crying in the street
Alms! Alms! For the down trodden
Beggars beg for help

Destiny

D

Future set in stone
Destiny is winter's fire
Its flame burns your fate

Heaven's Tears

H

Their tears fell like rain
Ten thousand angels crying
Crucifixion Day

Kettles and Conversation

K

Where home and hearth is
Kettles and conversation
Dreams are voiced here

Solace

S

Solace of the mind
Tranquility of the soul
In solace find peace

Haiku Nature

H

Generation gap
Playful youth, Death and dying
Winter Spring collide

Territorial siege
Weeds and daisies battle cry
A war is at hand

Pact made in springtime
Glorious new birth erupts
Love in the meadow

Geography search
Willows crying in the night
Where no one can see

Promised in summer
Seedlings fertilization
Kissed by sun and dew

Conquest in Autumn
Crunching sounds fall to the ground
Leaving winter trees

Invoked Spring's decree
Wild flowers burst into bloom
Fragrant aroma

Atrium, enter here
Beware guns are in the wood
Doe is on alert

Planet Colliding
Volcano erupts by night
Darkened skies today

Year ending in drought
Thirsty squirrels paw the lake bed
In desperation

First Place Blue Ribbon

Nancy Lee Shrader - Haiku: NATURE

Turtle's Vacation

T

Darkness all around
Turtle hidden in his shell
Keep away the world

Finding the courage
Turtle emerge from his shell
Joins the world today

He's in a frenzy
Turtle runs to catch the boat
Time to live again

All around the world
Turtle on a vacation
Swimming, diving too

Nocturnal Haiku

N

Nocturnal means night
Hunters and prey scurry here
Death sounds in the night

Mice scurry in fear
Quietly he stalks his prey
Who-o-o who-o-o cries the owl

Leopard stalks the wild
Crouching low he waits to strike
In silence he pounced

Jackal roams the bush
A scavenger by nature
Kills in dark of night

Australia's wild dogs
Was once domesticated
Dingoes hunt in packs

Raccoon dumpster dives
Nature's bandit of the woods
Rings around his tail

Bats in the belfry
Fluttering black wings takes flight
Brings fear to the night

Wolves howl at the moon
Before the hunting begins
Eyes glow in the dark

Day sleeps in burrow
Feasts at night on rotting flesh
Opossum hangs by tail

Sprays a pungent scent
Keeping predators away
Black and white the skunk

Hedgehog's spiny scales
He wears his suit of armor
Predators beware

Stripes upon its face
Kin to skunks and weasels too
Badger stalks the night

Frog on lily pad
Sings a croaking song by night
Long tongue catches flies

Twinkles on and off
Fireflies light up the night sky
Lightning in a jar

Glides from tree to tree
Flying squirrel takes flight by night
Stabilizing tail

Scurries though your house
Eyes glowing red in the dark
Mouse dwells inside walls

A sticky long tongue
Aardvark has a narrow snout
Eats termites and ants

Tiger instills fear
Feasts on deer and antelope
Endangered species

Man eating reptile
Swimming in the everglades
Alligator smiles

Giant man eater
Tropical anaconda
Squeezes life from prey

A small bandicoot
Endangered of extinction
Excavates its home

Anaconda kin
Is nocturnal by nature
Boa Constrictor

Has a spotted coat
Bob Cat, a fierce hunter
Cat of the prairie

Chirping in the night
Cricket sings a chirping song
Calling for its mate

Eater of plant life
Kangaroo's hop forty miles
Young live in its pouch

Cute Koala Bears
Dines on eucalyptus leaves
Cheek pouches store food

Creepy crawly legs
Tarantula creeps by night
Poison fangs sink deep

From a hollow log
Tasmanian Devil lurks
Devil carnivore

Swooping vampire bats
Lust for blood on vampire wing
We fear these creatures

Black footed ferret
Live in prairie dog burrows
There's not many left

Jaguars are wild cats
On endangered species' list
Are graceful swimmers

Carnivorous cat
Lynx from North America
Mostly nocturnal

Medium sized cat
It calls the rain forest home
Ocelots roam free

Lives inside your home
Nocturnal as all the rest
Purring, hear your cat

Cunning is the fox
Lives in woods and cities too
Has been urbanized

Fourth Place
Nancy Lee Shrader - Jackal

Fifth Place
Nancy Lee Shrader - Owl

Honorable Mention
Nancy Lee Shrader - Leopard

Honorable Mention
Nancy Lee Shrader – Fox

Second Place
Nancy Lee Shrader - Haiku Lightning In a Jar
November 19, 2008

About the Author

Nancy Lee resides in Beckley, West Virginia with her husband of almost forty years. She has three children and three grandchildren. She is author of three books *IS IT NOW? The End of Days! IS HE MESSIAH? Messianic Prophecies Revealed!* and *The Curse of Mayweather House* and has recently signed contracts for *The Haunting of Mayweather House, The Ghosts of Mayweather House, Mayweather House, The Evil's Revenge, Celestial Invasion* and just recently for her first book of poetry, *Haiku Smiles*. Nancy Lee also writes for Amazon.com. To her credit, she has twenty-one Shorts to date on the Amazon website. She is a member of the West Virginia Writers' Union, Appalachian Writers' Guild and belongs to a Writers' group at the Raleigh County Library.

I was born Nancy Lee Pilkington on January 5, 1948 to the late William Thomas Pilkington and Ora Estella Stone Pilkington. I married Dennis Shrader of Clarksburg in a church ceremony at St. Stephens Episcopal Church—where I am still a member. I have lived almost my entire life here in Beckley—with a brief time spent in Charleston while attending school, and a few years in Clarksburg when I was first married, but the rest of my sixty-one years were spent here in Beckley, where my husband and I raised three children, and buried a son who died at the age of three.

My writing career began many years before I typed the first word on my computer. It was my love for the written word—a love that had been lost over the years and only through a medical problem did this old love find a new place in my life. My love for reading began early in life—as a child I spent hours at the library reading of exciting people and faraway places. My favorite Author back then was Elisabeth Ogillvie—I read her books over and over— *Blueberry Summer* was my favorite. I also enjoyed the Nancy Drew and the Hardy Boys Mysteries, and of course the Little House Series.

However, those quiet hours in the Public Library came to an end on a sunny afternoon when my father bought our first color television, and a top-of-the-line antenna that turned in all directions—picking up five channels instead of the one that was pretty good and the other that was fuzzy. Reading took a back seat to the little box full of color. I hate to admit it, but I spent most of my adult life glued to the television screen—and not until recent years did my love for the written word find its way back into my life.

Once in high school, I tried my hand at writing, but failed miserably. It wasn't until I discovered the computer, and the program Word Perfect did my writing skills improve, but I'm getting ahead of my story. I didn't just one day pick up a book and began reading, rediscovering the pleasures of my youth. You see, I have a problem with short term memory loss, caused from a medication I was taking. It didn't happen all at once, but slowly over time—I was forgetting more and more. Then one day as I was writing a grocery list—I couldn't remember how to make a (k) in milk. Needless to say that got my attention. I didn't know what to do or where to turn—not wanting to face the hard truth—I had a very real problem.

Then one day I took an elderly friend, who was in the early stages of Alzheimer, to her doctor's appointment. The doctor gave her some advice that I adopted for myself. The doctor told my friend to read everything she could get her hands on, write letters, poetry—to just exercise her mind in order to slow the effects of the disease. You've heard the old saying, if you don't use it you'll lose it—well I took that doctor's advice to heart, and I'm here to tell you, the advice from that doctor has been a godsend. I'm now back to reading instead of watching television. My mind might not be at 100%, far from it, but it's better than it was three years ago. I still have problems, but my memory problems have been instrumental in the creation of IS IT NOW? The End of Days! Released March 6, 2006, IS HE MESSIAH? Messianic Prophecies Revealed! Released April 2007 and The Curse of Mayweather House, released April 2007. The second book in the Mayweather Series The Haunting of Mayweather House and the first in a three part series CELESTIAL INVASION, are coming in 2009.

ALL THINGS THAT MATTER PRESS ™

FOR MORE INFORMATION ON TITLES AVAILABLE
FROM ALL THINGS THAT MATTER PRESS, GO TO
http://allthingsthatmatterpress.com
or contact us at
allthingsthatmatterpress@gmail.com